JUSTIN BIEBER

CONTENTS

JUSTIN BIEBER

Official Annual 2012

century

Published By Century Books Limted,
Unit I, Upside Station Building,
Solsbro Road, Torquay, Devon, TQ2 6FD.
books@centurybooksltd.co.uk   Published 2011.

£7.99

JUST A REGULAR KID....

Justin Drew Bieber was born on March 1st 1994 in London, Ontario, Canada to Pattie Lynn Mallette and Jeremy Jack Bieber. Sadly, Justin's parents split up when he was just ten months old. After that Justin moved with his mum to a small town called Stratford.

Life wasn't easy – Pattie had to work several jobs to make ends meet – but Justin did have a loving upbringing.

He was very close to his grandparents Bruce and Diane Dale and was always encouraged to do his best. Like most youngsters, Justin loved sports like football and skateboarding. But in private he had another passion – music. Before he started school he was already playing the drums, piano and guitar!

Justin attended Jeanne Sauve Catholic School, where lessons were taught in French. However it was outside school at the ice hockey club that he met his best friends Chaz Somers and Ryan Butler.

Justin's life has changed completely since those early days, but he's still a down-to-earth dude whose family and friends mean the world to him. His mum, Pattie, is always by his side, even when he's on tour. Chaz and Ryan are still his best buds. To them he'll always be just Justin.

> " I was lucky. Along with a lot of other blessings, I got my family – just the way they are. "

> **I go back to Stratford to visit Grandpa and Grandma and my friends as often as I can and everybody treats me the same as always.**

> **My mum is a trip and she sacrificed everything for me.**

Justin
IN A NUTSHELL

NICKNAMES:
JBiebz, Biebz or JB

STAR SIGN:
Pisces

FAVOURITE COLOUR:
Purple

FAVOURITE ANIMAL:
Giraffe

YUMMIEST MEAL:
Spaghetti bolognese

MUSICAL LIKES:
Boys II Men, Michael Jackson

FAVOURITE BOOK:
Fledgling, a Jason Steed adventure by Mark A Cooper

GREATEST FEAR:
Being trapped in a lift

BIGGEST CELEBRITY CRUSH:
Beyoncé

IT'S GREAT TO BE
A Bieber Fan...

★ ...because if you love Justin then you're known as a 'Belieber'.

★ ...because you can never be too young or too old to heart JB. A three year old called Cody recently met Justin after a YouTube clip showing her crying over the star rocketed to 1.3 million hits! In Australia, a thirty-four-year-old forklift driver made the news with his own personalised Bieber car licence plates.

★ ...because you're among friends. It's impossible to measure exactly how many Beliebers there are in the world, but he has over 810,000 friends on My Space and nine million followers on Twitter.

★ ...because the way you feel has a name. It's called 'Bieber Fever'.

JUSTIN
And Me

BACKSTAGE PASS

STICK A PICTURE OF YOURSELF IN HERE

FIRST NAME

SURNAME

DATE OF BIRTH

AGE

NOW YOU'RE A TRUE BELIEBER, JUSTIN WOULD BE HONOURED TO HANG OUT WITH YOU! FILL YOUR DETAILS INTO THIS BACKSTAGE PASS – DON'T FORGET TO STICK IN YOUR PHOTO OR YOU'LL NEVER GET PAST SECURITY. AFTERWARDS, HAVE FUN PLANNING YOUR FIRST MEETING WITH THE MAN HIMSELF...

Justin and I are so similar. We both like...

The thing I admire most about Justin is...

My favourite Justin Bieber track has got to be...

Justin would love the way I...

If we met, I'd say...

And I'd definitely wear...

We'd have such a great time hanging out! I'd take him...

NOT JUST A PRETTY FACE

DID YOU KNOW THAT AS WELL AS BEING SUPER CUTE AND AN AMAZING SINGER, JUSTIN IS ALSO A TALENTED MUSICIAN?

Drums

The drums were JB's first instrument and his first love. He started banging out beats on pots, pans and tabletops when he was just two years old. When he reached four his mum bought him his first drum kit. At first Justin's talent was much bigger than he was – once while drumming at a local fair the compère joked, "Well I see you guys brought a drum set, but where's the drummer?" Nowadays, he's all grown up. Justin can be seen over the cymbals and he loves to showcase his skills with sick drum solos on stage.

SAY WHAT?

"Mum always says I was all about the beat. I suppose that makes sense. Before anything else you gotta have rhythm."

"With drums you can kind of let out emotion."

Piano

JB began tinkling the ivories at the tender age of five. His mum couldn't afford to pay for lessons, so he climbed up onto the piano stool and taught himself by picking out notes and experimenting.

SAY WHAT?

"I couldn't read music – I was just beginning to read books... but I knew what I wanted the music to sound like. I could feel it when the chords and melody didn't fit together, the way you can feel it when your shoes are on the wrong foot."

Guitar

Justin began playing the guitar as soon as he was big enough to get his hands around the neck. He practised while waiting for his supper, or when he was grounded in his room for being cheeky. Soon he was playing knockout renditions of rock songs like 'Knockin' On Heaven's Door' by Bob Dylan and 'Smoke On The Water' by Deep Purple. Justin still loves to learn. After seeing the film *August Rush*, which stars young Brit actor Freddie Highmore as a music prodigy, Justin taught himself to play slap guitar – lying the guitar flat and slapping it to make chords *and* a beat.

SAY WHAT?

"If you know the basic form of five or six barre chords, you can play pretty much any song in the universe."

"I played guitar because it was fun and by the time I was eight or nine, I was all right."

"Until you build calluses on your fingertips, it feels like razor blades. That probably discourages a lot of people."

"It wasn't an issue of learning it exactly: it was more as if the music soaked in through my skin."

Trumpet

Justin took up the trumpet at school, but hadn't been playing long when he was catapulted to fame as a singer. He recently treated fans to a few bars of 'Mary Had A Little Lamb' on French radio show NRJ, but he was a bit rusty and admitted he hadn't played in a long time.

SAY WHAT?

"I'm pretty good. I'm not like, amazing, but I can play it."

Learn The LYRICS

'Fess up! You're always crooning to the latest Bieber tune – in the shower, tidying your room, to your reflection in the mirror using a hairbrush as a microphone. Are you word perfect or a la la let down?
Do you hum like a dummy or can you sing like a winner?
The lyrics below are each missing a key word. Can you complete them? Choose from the list at the bottom of the page.

1. Are we an ....? Girl, quit playin',

   'We're just friends', what are you sayin'?
   _____

2. I never thought I could feel this ....,

   I never thought that I could feel this free.
   _____

3. How many I told yous and start overs,

   And .... have you cried on before.
   _____

4. When I met you girl, my .... went knock knock,

   Now them butterflies in my stomach won't stop stop.
   _____

5. For you I'd write a symphony I'd tell the violin,

   It's time to sink or ...., watch him play for ya.
   _____

6. There's a .... that I've been chasing,

   Want so badly for it to be reality.
   _____

POWER

SWIM

HEART

ITEM

DREAM

SHOULDERS

14

The lyrics on the page opposite are taken from some of Justin's greatest hits. Slide your Bieber knowledge up a level by matching the lyrics with the back-to-front song titles below. Reverse the letters and write each tune the correct way round in the spaces provided. Now draw a line to match each song title to the rhymes on the facing page.

A. REVEN YAS REVEN

_ _ _ _ _ _   _ _ _   _ _ _ _ _

B. EVOL OT YDOBEMOS

_ _ _ _ _ _ _ _   _ _   _ _ _ _

C. YBAB

_ _ _ _

D. OG UOY TEL REVEN

_ _ _ _ _   _ _ _   _ _ _   _ _

E. EMIT ENO

_ _ _   _ _ _ _

F. LRIG YLENOL

_ _ _ _ _ _   _ _ _ _

WOLF PACK
WORDSEARCH

JUSTIN CALLS HIS ENTOURAGE HIS 'WOLF PACK' – THE SMALL, TRUSTED GROUP OF PEOPLE WHO LOOK AFTER THE STAR. CAN YOU FIND EACH OF THEIR NAMES HIDDEN IN THE GRID BELOW? GRAB A PEN AND START SEARCHING FOR WOLVES, CHECKING EACH PERSON OFF THE LIST BELOW AS YOU GO. YOU'LL NEED TO LOOK CAREFULLY, THE NAMES COULD BE RUNNING IN ANY DIRECTION!

U	G	F	E	A	B	C	R	Y	E
S	C	O	O	T	E	R	H	P	E
H	J	O	M	A	M	A	J	A	N
E	B	E	D	I	Q	U	K	T	X
R	Y	A	N	G	O	O	D	T	A
U	S	A	Y	N	A	W	P	I	R
S	D	W	V	X	Y	N	N	E	K
C	H	A	Z	S	O	M	E	R	S
R	E	L	T	U	B	N	A	Y	R
Y	J	A	M	A	I	C	A	N	K

- ☐ SCOOTER (MANAGER)
- ☐ PATTIE (MUM)
- ☐ RYAN GOOD (STYLIST AND SWAGGER COACH)
- ☐ USHER (MENTOR)
- ☐ MAMA JAN (VOICE COACH)
- ☐ JENNY (TUTOR)
- ☐ KENNY (BODYGUARD)
- ☐ DAN (GUITARIST)
- ☐ CHAZ SOMERS (FRIEND)
- ☐ RYAN BUTLER (FRIEND)
- ☐ JAMAICA (CHOREOGRAPHER)

A to Z of JUSTIN BIEBER

A is for Atlanta, the US city Justin moved to when he kicked off his recording career.

B is for Busking. Before he was famous, JB spent many weekends playing for passers-by on the steps of his town's local theatre.

C IS FOR CHECKED SHIRTS — PART OF JB'S TRADEMARK LOOK.

D is for Dancing. Justin has some mean moves including 'the dougie', which he often performs on stage.

E IS FOR EDDIE'S ATTIC. THIS IS THE LIVE MUSIC VENUE IN ATLANTA WHERE JUSTIN PERFORMED HIS FIRST SHOWCASE.

F is for French. Justin parle très bien français!

G is for Girls. The Bieber totally loves the ladies.

H IS FOR HAIR. WHETHER IT'S THE TRADEMARK SWISH OR HIS CURRENT CROP, HIS DO IS ALWAYS COOL.

I is for Ice Hockey – JB's favourite sport.

J IS FOR JustBeats, THE HEADPHONES BY DR DRE THAT JUSTIN ENDORSES.

K is for Kindness. A compassionate Piscean by nature, the generous star donated more than £18,000 from his concert ticket sales in Nashville to the Tennessee Flood Recovery effort.

L is for Ludacris, the artist who featured alongside Justin on 'Baby'.

M is for MVP. JB was named most valuable player during a recent NBA All-Star celebrity basketball game in Los Angeles.

N is for *Never Say Never*, the movie of Justin's meteoric rise to stardom.

O is for 'One Time', JB's first kicking single.

P is for Punking. Bieber is a practical joker who loves to play tricks on his friends.

Q is for Questions. Justin loves interviews, especially when he's asked serious questions about his musical tastes and influences.

R is for Rollercoaster. JB is a big fan of the scary rides and hit the headlines when he rode Behemoth at Six Flags Magic Mountain theme park in LA.

S is for 'Someday' by Justin Bieber. Did you know that the star has launched his own gorgeous perfume for girls who want to smell good?

T is for Tattoos. JB has three — a seagull, the word 'Jesus' in Hebrew and a star on his elbow.

JUSTIN ALWAYS LOOKS HIS ALPHA-BEST! HERE HE IS SMILING AND SMOULDERING ON A RECENT PHOTOSHOOT.

U is for 'U Smile'. This soulful ballad was co-written by Justin and loved by critics and fans alike.

V is for Vicks Steam Inhaler. The machine, which helps his voice, features on his backstage 'rider' (the list of items a star would like to have in their dressing room).

W is for Willow Smith. Justin invited the hair-whipping songstress to support him on the European leg of his world tour.

X is for the XL Center in Hartford, Connecticut. This was the enormous venue for the first show of Justin's 'My World' tour.

Y is for YouTube. The awesome site got JB noticed, hooked him a manager and brought him global recognition.

Z is for Zamboni, the machine used to smooth an ice rink. The young, hockey-mad Justin used to dream of riding around the rink on one during half-time at games.

The JOURNEY To STARDOM

Part One

He's gone from zero to hero in the blink of an eye. But where did it all begin for Justin and exactly how did he manage to climb so quickly to the dizzying heights of mega-stardom?

The journey began in January 2007, when a twelve year old entered a local talent contest called 'The Stratford Star'. Back then he had no desire to be famous, he just wanted to see how it would feel to perform in front of an audience. He liked the sound of the grand prize – a microphone that could record onto a computer. Incredibly, the gifted youngster only placed third, but his performances of Matchbox 20's '3AM', Alicia Keys' 'Fallin'' and Aretha Franklin's 'Respect' were so well received that his proud mum posted the clips on YouTube.

These were the first of many Bieber posts on the site, which has been both a launch pad and a vital marketing tool for the star. At the time, however, neither Justin nor his mum had any idea of the impact these home videos would have.

Encouraged by his competition success, Justin began busking on the steps of the Stratford Theatre most weekends. He'd sit with his guitar, strumming and singing tunes like the Rascal Flatt song 'Sarah Beth'. Before long he was making some serious money. A string of impressed girls started dropping phone numbers in his guitar case, too!

Justin saved up all his busking money, hoping to take his mum on holiday to Disney World. His savings scheme didn't quite work out as planned. Fate intervened in the form of a music industry talent scout named Scooter...

READ MORE OF JUSTIN'S STORY ON PAGE 26!

THE BIG BIEBER QUIZ
LEVEL ONE

Welcome to the Big Bieber Quiz – the ultimate place to prove your super-fan status! Level one is for Bieber beginners. All you've got to do is answer true or false to the twenty statements below. Grab a pencil, switch on your fave Bieber track and get ticking! When you've finished, turn to page 44 and graduate to level two.

QUESTION 1
Justin is American.

TRUE ☐   FALSE ☐

QUESTION 2
He grew up in Stratford-upon-Avon, England.

TRUE ☐   FALSE ☐

QUESTION 3
He can play the guitar, trumpet, drums and piano.

TRUE ☐   FALSE ☐

QUESTION 4
His mum's name is Pam.

TRUE ☐   FALSE ☐

QUESTION 5
His dad's name is Jeremy.

TRUE ☐   FALSE ☐

QUESTION 6
His mentor is Justin Timberlake.

TRUE ☐   FALSE ☐

JUSTIN BIEBER

22

QUESTION 7

His favourite sport is horse racing.

TRUE ☐   FALSE ☐

QUESTION 8

His manager's name is Scott 'Scooter' Braun.

TRUE ☐   FALSE ☐

QUESTION 9

He once entered a talent contest called 'American Idol'.

TRUE ☐   FALSE ☐

QUESTION 10

His first single was called 'Baby'.

TRUE ☐   FALSE ☐

QUESTION 11

He got his first drum kit when he was four.

TRUE ☐   FALSE ☐

QUESTION 12

He likes to wear checked shirts.

TRUE ☐   FALSE ☐

QUESTION 13

His favourite food is sausage and mash.

TRUE ☐   FALSE ☐

QUESTION 14

His best friends are called Ryan and Chaz.

TRUE ☐   FALSE ☐

POLAROID 32

JBIEBZ TINKLING THE IVORIES.
WHAT OTHER INSTRUMENTS DOES HE PLAY?

QUESTION 15

His star sign is Sagittarius.

TRUE ☐   FALSE ☐

QUESTION 16

His birthday is 1st March.

TRUE ☐   FALSE ☐

QUESTION 17

His middle name is Drew.

TRUE ☐   FALSE ☐

QUESTION 18

Bieber Fans are called Beliebers.

TRUE ☐   FALSE ☐

QUESTION 19

He once broke his arm live on stage.

TRUE ☐   FALSE ☐

QUESTION 20

His eyes are blue.

TRUE ☐   FALSE ☐

?

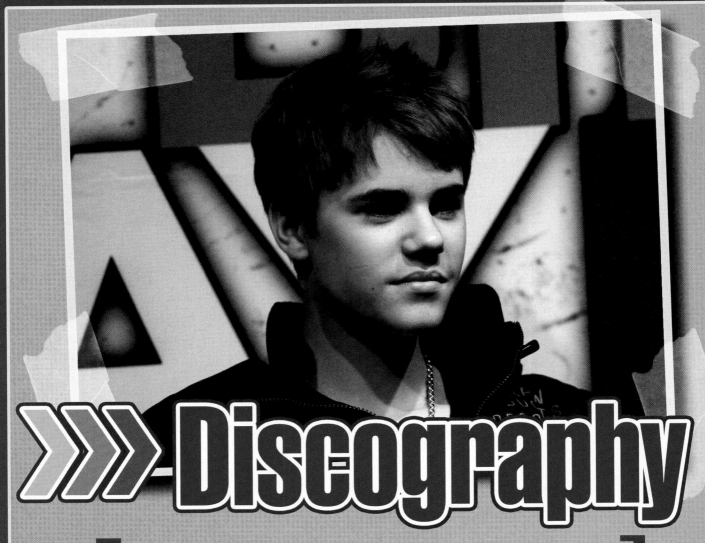

>>> Discography

JB is one busy Bieber. So far the star has released four knockout albums and ten sizzling singles! Check out this timeline – have you downloaded all of Justin's greatest hits?

ONE TIME

TYPE:	Single
RELEASE DATE:	7th July 2009

ONE LESS LONELY GIRL

TYPE:	Single
RELEASE DATE:	6th October 2009

LOVE ME

TYPE:	Single
RELEASE DATE:	26th October 2009

FAVORITE GIRL

TYPE:	Single
RELEASE DATE:	3rd November 2009

MY WORLD

TYPE:	Album
RELEASE DATE:	17th November 2009

BABY FEAT. LUDACRIS

TYPE:	Single
RELEASE DATE:	19th January 2010

NEVER LET YOU GO

TYPE:	Single
RELEASE DATE:	2nd March 2010

U SMILE

TYPE:	Single
RELEASE DATE:	16th March 2010

MY WORLD 2.0

TYPE:	Album
RELEASE DATE:	23rd March 2010

SOMEBODY TO LOVE FEAT. USHER

TYPE:	Single
RELEASE DATE:	22nd June 2010

NEVER SAY NEVER FEAT. JAYDEN SMITH

TYPE:	Single
RELEASE DATE:	8th June 2010

MY WORLDS ACOUSTIC

TYPE:	Album
RELEASE DATE:	26th November 2010

BABY (GLEE SEASON TWO)

TYPE:	Single on Album
RELEASE DATE:	11th February 2011

NEVER SAY NEVER – THE REMIXES

TYPE:	Album
RELEASE DATE:	14th February 2011

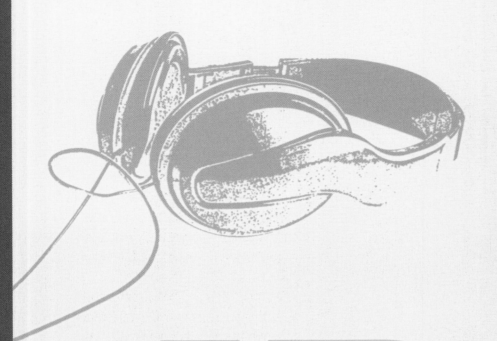

The JOURNEY To STARDOM

Part Two

BY NOW A BRILLIANT BUSKER AND STAR IN HIS HOMETOWN OF STRATFORD, READ ON TO DISCOVER HOW JB GOT HIS BIG BREAK...

One day in summer 2007, Scott 'Scooter' Braun was browsing the internet when he came across clips of Justin performing on YouTube. As well as his mum's movies, impressed tourists had uploaded films of JB busking, too. The kid's appeal and growing fan base was obvious. Thousands of people had already watched and commented on the clips.

Scooter Braun decided he'd seen enough – he needed to meet JB in person! He managed to track down Justin's mum through the local education authority, persuading the school to pass Pattie his number. At first, Justin's mum didn't call back. After a while, she decided to dial the stranger from a blocked number just to get him off her back.

But in one phone chat Scooter managed to persuade Pattie that he had seen something special in Justin. Pattie and Justin decided to fly to Atlanta to meet Scooter and talk things through.

Justin and his mum boarded their first-ever flight on an aeroplane in autumn 2007. Even then, the young musician still had no idea of the much greater journey he was about to embark upon...

**TURN TO PAGE 34
TO FIND OUT WHAT
HAPPENED WHEN
JUSTIN MET SCOOTER!**

CLEVER

COLLABORATIONS

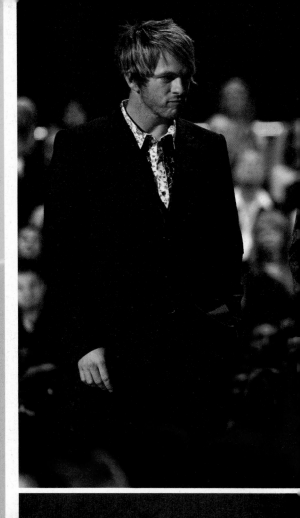

Justin is known for his versatility – making cool collaborations with the brightest stars in the music industry. From country to R&B via pop, hip-hop and rap, there's no genre that he won't try on for size! It's even rumoured that the megastar has been spotted at P.Diddy's studio. Here's the lowdown on some of the major artists that Biebz has already worked with, plus the inside track on what they thought of each other.

CHRIS BROWN ›

JB has always been a fan and sang Brown's hit 'With You' in his world-famous YouTube clip. Now the two share mutual professional respect. The R&B star featured on JB's track 'Up' before Justin returned the favour by featuring on 'Next to you' on Brown's album 'Fame'. Brown even made a surprise appearance on stage with Bieber in Sydney!

Bieber on Brown:
"We just talk about regular stuff, nothing too crazy. Just like, staying humble and remembering that God got us in this position, so always make sure to just bless him and praise him."

Brown on Bieber:
"Being able to collab with him was great. He's a young, energetic cat, so being able to work with him, with the fan base he has, was incredible. I know a lot of little girls are going to love this record."

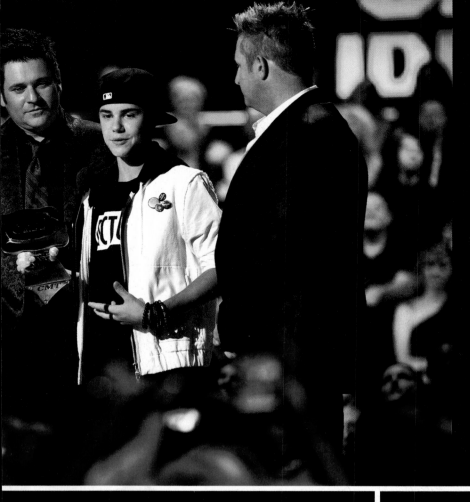

❮ RASCAL FLATTS

The country group worked with Justin on the number 'It Should Have Been Me'. Their hard work was rewarded when the performers won the 2011 Country Music Television award for best collaborative video.

Bieber on Flatts:
"I love Rascal Flatts and I'm honoured that they are making music with me."

Flatts singer Gary LeVox on Bieber:
"You know what? I was really impressed by him. One, because of his musical gifts. Plus, him singing live was really great. Plus he's a great dancer... and his knowledge of music... but his character was the thing I was interested in seeing. And man, he's just a great kid. My hat's off to his parents, you know, you can tell he's had a great upbringing."

⌄ KANYE WEST

Justin's collaboration with the legend that is Kanye began with a mutual love-in on Twitter, with West exclaiming that he was spending a lazy Sunday morning in his 'crib' listening to Bieber's 'Runaway Love'.

Bieber on West:
"He reproduced the 'Runaway' joint, and I'm really excited. He's such a cool guy, and he's just really laid back and nice. It's funny, because he doesn't even use a phone; he just sends email. It's so crazy. I'm like, 'How can you not use a phone?'"

West on Bieber:
To accompany a pic of himself with Biebz in his studio West posted on Twitter, "My new beat protégé!"

29

CLEVER COLLABORATIONS

⌃ LUDACRIS

The pair were introduced by Justin's manager Scooter, before collaborating on JB's massive hit 'Baby'.

Bieber on Ludacris:
"I've taught Ludacris everything he knows about girls."

Ludacris on Bieber:
"As soon as they sent me the record, I'm a fan of music period and I knew it would be an instant hit, so I got on that thing man."

SEAN KINGSTON ❯

The hip-hop and reggae singer joined forces with JB to record 'Eenie Meenie'. Both artists loved the experience, getting on really well. So when Kingston was almost killed in a jet-ski crash in May 2011, JB tweeted prayers for his recovery.

Bieber on Kingston:
"Got my friend Sean Kingston in my prayers tonight. A true friend and big bro. Please keep him in your prayers tonight as well."

Kingston on Bieber:
"Me and Justin have been friends for the past two years. So one day he was like 'yo' and said he wanted to do a record with me. I was like 'let's do it, I'm ready!' and he came down over the Superbowl weekend and slept over at my house. We banged out a couple of records and 'Eenie Meenie' was definitely the most special one."

JADEN SMITH ❯

JB and JS met when they paired up to record the theme tune for Jaden's movie – the remake of *The Karate Kid*. Since then, they've hung out with each other from time to time. The pals both performed with Usher at the Grammys and Jaden has also appeared on stage at Justin's concerts.

Bieber on Smith:
"Right now, the best thing is just being teenagers having fun doing what we love. We're just staying ourselves and remaining humble."

Smith on Bieber:
"It was great, he's amazing. Justin is great to work with and the coolest kid."

MILEY CYRUS

Snaps of the pair having lunch together got everyone talking, but both Miley and Justin have been quick to quash rumours that they're dating. The friends did however hook up to record 'Overboard' live at Madison Square Garden. Since then, Justin only has good things to say about working with Miley.

Bieber on Cyrus:
"It was great. She was really nice and everything."

Cyrus on Bieber:
"We're strictly friends. He's very cute though, I totally get it. We don't talk about business and stuff, we talk about anything but. He's from Canada and I've been there with my dad – I like Canada a lot."

AND THERE'S EVEN MORE...

Justin can't resist getting his talented pals up on stage. Willow Smith, Boyz II Men, Selena Gomez and Joel Madden of Good Charlotte are just some of the famous faces that have performed alongside JBiebz.

Who would you like to see JB duet with next time around? Imagine a stellar showbiz combination, then write it in here.

I would love to see Justin sing with:

....

ALL ABOUT
USHER

"There's a lot Scooter can tell me and I trust him, but he doesn't know what it's like for me dealing with living in the spotlight the way Usher does."

Usher on Bieber:
"What he's been able to accomplish in a short amount of time is amazing. I'm kinda speechless. It only happens once in a lifetime that an artist will have that amount of success."

"From the moment I looked at him online I knew that there was something very special. And the world would definitely enjoy it. I wanted to be able to help him tell his story in a way that will last forever."

"At times the relationship goes in the direction of father, but more so brother and uncle. We all need supporters that ultimately care. It's not just business for me. He's someone I care a lot about and I invested in the long-haul of his life, not just these moments of success in music."

"I always tell him, while this is great, don't get too caught up in this moment... don't lose the essence of who you are."

No talk of collaborations can fail to big up Usher – JB's mentor extraordinaire! As well as offering career support and guidance to Justin, Usher has become a great personal friend. The talented R&B star's own record sales top 45 million, but he was bowled over by Justin's talent from the first time he heard him sing. He was even more impressed that JB was bold enough to audition using Usher's own track 'U Got It Bad'.

Since then, Justin and Usher's relationship has gone from strength to strength. Now the pals regularly hang out and perform together. From treating manager Scooter to a private show at his 30th birthday party to working Usher's smash hit 'OMG' at the Grammys, the pair always kill it on stage.

Bieber on Usher:
"We made the decision to go forward with Usher and I've never doubted it for a second. I'm the luckiest guy on Earth to have him as my wingman."

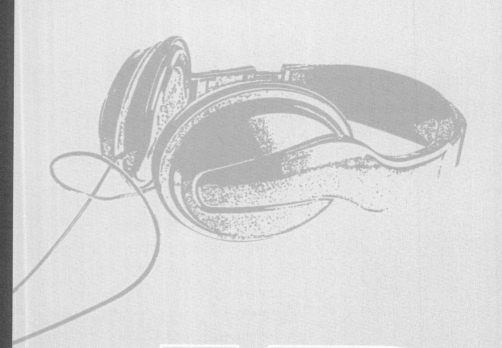

The JOURNEY To STARDOM

Part Three

Scooter Braun met Justin and his mum at the airport in Atlanta, and then whizzed the new arrivals straight over to meet record producer Jermain Dupri. As they were crossing the car park at the studios, Justin spotted Usher. JB couldn't resist rushing over to say hi to the star who would later become his mentor.

During that first visit Scooter wanted Justin to relax and get to know him. The pair played video games and hung out, with the producer soon gaining Pattie's trust, too. By the time they left, the group had the beginnings of a working relationship.

The plan was that Justin should continue making and posting videos on YouTube to cement his following. This is exactly what happened – the hits recorded on his rendition of Chris Brown's song 'With You' soon tipped a million!

Scooter talked to the record labels, but they still weren't interested in this unknown kid with a voice. The manager didn't lose faith. He knew it would only take one person to listen, really listen, to Justin, to get the break they needed.

Finally, in February 2008, Scooter managed to get both Justin Timberlake and Usher to meet JB. The two Justins got along great, but after Biebz sang 'You Got It Bad' for Usher, a winning partnership was born.

In April 2008, Scooter and Usher took Justin to New York to sign a record deal at Island Def Jam. That autumn, Justin and his mum moved to Atlanta to begin honing his vocals and laying down tracks.

JUSTIN'S INCREDIBLE JOURNEY
CONTINUES ON PAGE 42!

NEVER
SAY NEVER

THE MOVIE

IF YOU HAVEN'T SEEN JB'S FIRST OUTING ON THE SILVER SCREEN… WHAT HAVE YOU BEEN DOING? GET YOURSELF DOWN TO YOUR NEAREST CINEMA TO CHECK OUT THE BIEBZ DOING THE BIZ IN GLORIOUS TECHNICOLOR! HERE'S JUST A TASTER OF WHAT YOU CAN EXPECT…

IN IT OR BIN IT?

Study this list of Justin's incredible on-screen antics. Can you work out which are really featured in the movie and which aren't? Put a tick or cross in the box beside each phrase.

1. Firing silly string during a photo-shoot ☐
2. Unwrapping a bongo and a dart game ☐
3. Petting lion cubs in central park zoo ☐
4. Checking out some dead, stuffed animals – including a wolf that is missing a leg ☐
5. Juggling melons ☐
6. Doing the tango with Rhianna ☐
7. Praying over pizza ☐
8. Playing drums on a chair top ☐
9. Manhandling a giant cardboard cut-out of himself ☐
10. Shaving Ryan's hair ☐

11. Playing air-guitar with his shirt off in his dressing room ☐
12. Giving a young violinist playing on the steps of the theatre where he used to busk a motivational pep talk ☐
13. Piloting his own private jet ☐
14. Knitting a scarf with his grandma ☐
15. Scoring a basket from the half way line ☐
16. Hugging his mum and his grandad ☐
17. Playing tennis with plastic dinner plates ☐
18. Getting down with his security guard ☐
19. Swimming naked in a lake ☐
20. Getting soaked by a bucket of water ☐

WHO SAID IT?

Read these memorable quotes from *Never Say Never* then study the name checks beneath them. Now draw a line to connect the quote to the person who spoke it. Be warned, however, some people may have had more than one thing to say!

1. "Now that we don't see each other really like any more, we just cherish the time we have together." ☐

2. "You can't go out until you clean your room, OK?" ☐

3. "Justin is sitting on the bus and he's not moving, I think he's dehydrated from sitting in the sun all day yesterday..." ☐

4. "You really have to be more cautious, when you do have down-time." ☐

5. "So which one of you girls wants to make out with me right now, 3D?" ☐

6. "Thank you Lord for this pizza, this cheese, pineapple, bacon, pepperoni and thank you too Hawaiian people for making this pizza." ☐

7. "Where does that talent come from? Man you gotta get that kid a kit." ☐

8. "I just never thought of it as being anything other than for fun." ☐

9. "Ladies and Gentlemen, introducing to you, Island Def Jam Recording Artist Justin Bieber, get ready because he's going to be big. Ain't that right Justin?" ☐

10. "There is not a DJ that can say they have met Justin Bieber and he's not won people over." ☐

☐ **Mama Jan**
(Justin's voice coach)

☐ **Justin Bieber**

☐ **Usher**

☐ **Nathan McKay**
(Justin's neighbour)

☐ **Pattie Mallette**
(Justin's mum)

☐ **Scooter**

☐ **Diane Dale**
(Justin's grandma)

☐ **Chaz Somers**

girls:
ACCORDING TO JUSTIN

Ever asked yourself what Justin really thinks about girls? As the hottest star on the planet, he's met and been propositioned by more than most teens! Here's the pop sensation's verdict on girls, love and romance – all in JB's own words.

ON GIRLY STYLE:

"Uggs are ugly. I think big sunglasses are kind of overrated. I like big sunglasses, but not those huge round ones."

ON BEING MOBBED BY FEMALE FANS:

"I'm a really claustrophobic person to begin with. I hate elevators, especially crammed elevators. So I think it's very scary when girls are all around me and I can't go anywhere. At the same time, I guess I got to get used to it, you know what I mean?"

ON FIRST DATES:

"I took her to King's – a buffet restaurant. Yes, I wore a white shirt. Yes, I got spaghetti. It wasn't a big trauma, though. This girl was a friend, and she's pretty cool. We laughed about it."

ON FAMOUS CRUSHES:

"I have crushes, but they're all too old. I went up to give Beyoncé a hug at the Grammys and Jay-Z said, 'Watch out buddy!' He was kidding, but you know..."

"I sang to Nicole Scherzinger from the Pussycat Dolls. That was an amazing moment... it was hard to take my eyes off of her because she's so gorgeous."

ON VALENTINES DAY:

"I have one person I'll be sending flowers to and that's my mum. She's been there since the beginning and has given up a lot for me, I'm very blessed to have her."

ON ROMANCE:

"I think that being a gentleman is what matters; taking them out to a nice dinner, open the doors, stuff like that. Flowers are great, but love is better."

The rumour mill spins way faster when you're famous! Here are some of the completely crazy stories that have turned up online about our guy Biebz. Only one of the ten rumours on this page is actually true. Can you cut through the hype and circle the correct one?

Say What?

1. He has joined a religious cult called the Illuminati.

2. He's actually a girl in disguise.

3. He's working on a film project with Jaden Smith's dad, Will Smith.

4. Rapper Asher Roth is his brother.

5. He's going to be starting school in a city near you very soon.

6. Action movie legend Chuck Norris is his real father.

7. He is dating US reality show star Kim Kardashian.

8. He takes special pills to stop his voice from breaking.

9. He recently got arrested and sent to prison for molesting a fan.

10. He snubbed Kanye West's offer to work together.

Crazy For CANADA

Justin is a proud Canadian through and through. He's not alone – the country also gave us the talents of Avril Lavigne and Shania Twain, plus actors Keanu Reeves and Mike Myers. Here are twenty fun facts to help you swot up on your idol's homeland.

1 Ice hockey is Canada's national winter sport. The national sport during the summer months is lacrosse, a team game played with a ball and a netted stick.

2 CANADIANS CONSUME MORE MACARONI CHEESE THAN ANY OTHER NATION ON EARTH.

3 The country's icon is the beaver, but the maple leaf is more widely used as an emblem.

4 The nation's motto is 'From sea to sea'. It's a good choice given that Canada is surrounded by three vast oceans – the Pacific, the Atlantic and the Arctic. It has the longest coastline of any country in the world.

5 CANADA HAS HOSTED THE OLYMPIC GAMES THREE TIMES. ITS SHORES HAVE BEEN THE VENUE FOR THE SUMMER GAMES IN 1976 AND THE WINTER GAMES IN BOTH 1988 AND 2010.

6 JOHN CABOT WAS THE FIRST EXPLORER TO REACH CANADA IN 1497.

7 *Canadian metropolis Montreal is home to a climate-controlled underground city, a complex network of shops, restaurants and tunnels that stretch for more than 32 kilometres!*

8 A staggering 80% of the world's maple syrup supply is produced within Canada's borders, and of that, 93% is produced in Quebec. The country produces over 7 million gallons a year!

9 Canada is the second largest country in the world, only beaten in size by Russia.

10 QUEEN ELIZABETH II IS THE CANADIAN HEAD OF STATE.

11 Canada is known as the home of large animals like the moose, the grizzly bear and the polar bear, but it is also home to around 55,000 species of insects.

12 *The official languages of Canada are English and French.*

13 MANY FAMOUS AUTHORS HAVE COME FROM CANADA, INCLUDING LUCY MAUD MONTGOMERY, WHO WROTE *ANNE OF GREEN GABLES*.

14 THE WORD 'CANADA' COMES FROM THE ST. LAWRENCE-IROQUOIAN WORD FOR VILLAGE OR SETTLEMENT.

15 The West Edmonton Mall in Edmonton, Alberta, was once the largest shopping mall on the planet. It now ranks fifth, although it still contains the world's biggest indoor amusement park.

16 *A black bear cub from Canada named Winnipeg ('Winnie' for short) was donated to London Zoo in 1915. Winnie became a favourite of Christopher Robin Milne and inspired the stories written by his father. A.A. Milne's children's books starred a bear called Winnie the Pooh.*

17 Canadian winter temperatures can fall as low as -40°C, with snow covering some parts of the country for nearly six months of the year!

18 ONE TENTH OF THE WORLD'S FORESTS ARE IN CANADA. TREES COVER AROUND HALF OF THE COUNTRY.

19 *Canada is home to the longest street in the world. Yonge Street in Ontario starts at Lake Ontario then runs north to the Minnesota border, covering 2,000 kilometres.*

20 The comic 'Superman' was created by Canadian Joe Shuster, born in Toronto in 1914.

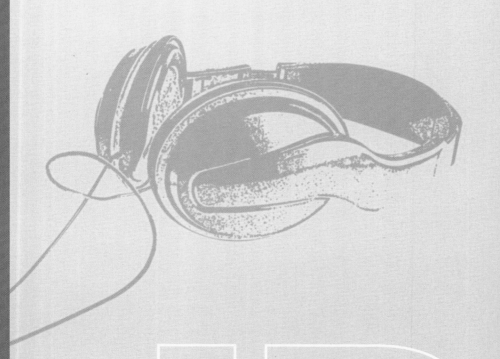

The JOURNEY To STARDOM

Part Four

Getting signed was a huge deal for Justin, but in reality it was just the beginning. The foundations of a fanbase were there, but now it was time to polish this rough diamond until he shone brightly enough to dazzle the world.

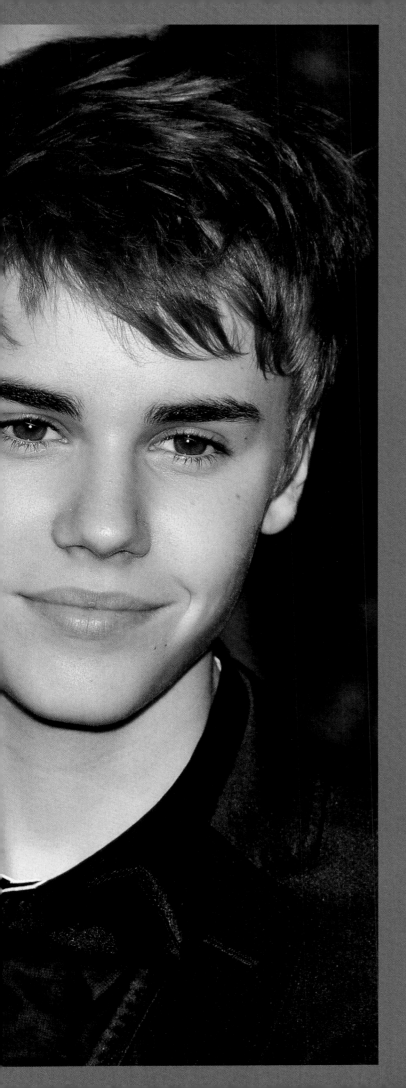

In Atlanta, Usher hooked Justin up with voice coach Jan Smith, aka Mama Jan. Together they worked on a song called 'Common Denominator' to debut at a famous venue called Eddie's Attic.

After Justin had sung his heart out at Eddie's Attic, L.A. Reid and Usher agreed that he was ready to start recording. They decided on a dozen songs plus some bonus tracks that would be divided between two albums – 'My World' and 'My World 2.0'.

Next Scooter organised for Justin to visit as many radio stations in the US as possible, generating interest in his debut single 'One Time'. With the help of the Biebz's tweeting and Facebook posting, the video for the track went viral. Within two days it was the second most-viewed video on iTunes!

'One Time' shot to number 14 in the US Charts, only kept from a higher position by the death of Michael Jackson. Since then the awesome combination of Justin's talent, Usher's guidance and Scooter's dedication to PR have seen JB's star continue to soar. 'My World' has now gone platinum and 'Baby', the debut single from 'My World 2.0' reached the top ten in eight countries.

He's achieved fame and fortune in such a brief time, but it seems that Justin still has so much more to give us. What will the pop sensation do next? Stay connected, watch and enjoy.

Bieber FOREVER!

THE BIG BIEBER QUIZ

LEVEL TWO

Blossoming Beliebers won't be fazed by the next level of our JB challenge! Now that you've passed level one, you're ready to delve a little deeper into the recesses of your pop knowledge. Find a pen and tick the answers that feel right, then check your answers on page 92.

QUESTION 1

For Justin's 16th birthday, Usher bought him a...

A. A Land Rover ○

B. A Range Rover ○

C. A dog named Rover ○

QUESTION 2

Justin has recently been dating...

A. Selena Gomez from *Wizards of Waverley Place* ○

B. Vanessa Hudgens from *High School Musical* ○

C. Miranda Cosgrave from *iCarly* ○

JUSTIN BIEBER

QUESTION 6

Justin has two half siblings called...

A. Jaxon and Jazmyn ◯

B. Ryan and Chaz ◯

C. Willow and Jaden ◯

QUESTION 7

Justin auditioned for Usher by singing his song...

A. 'My Way' ◯

B. 'OMG' ◯

C. 'U Got It Bad' ◯

QUESTION 3

The star who recently impersonated Justin on TV show *Saturday Night Live* was...

A. Taylor Swift ◯

B. Miley Cyrus ◯

C. Jennette McCurdy ◯

QUESTION 4

Justin's world tour was called...

A. Bieberland ◯

B. My World ◯

C. Bieber Nation ◯

QUESTION 5

When Justin went on holiday with his grandparents, they enjoyed...

A. Meeting Mickey Mouse and friends at Disney World, USA ◯

B. Seeing the sights in Paris, France ◯

C. Fishing at Star Lake, Canada ◯

QUESTION 8

The ice hockey team that Justin supports is called...

A. Toronto Maple Leafs ◯

B. Calgary Flames ◯

C. Vancouver Canucks ◯

QUESTION 9

Justin suffers from...

A. Agoraphobia ◯

B. Claustrophobia ◯

C. Arachnophobia ◯

QUESTION 10

JB's hit 'Baby' featured...

A. Ludacris ◯

B. Chris Brown ◯

C. Sean Kingston ◯

When you've answered all ten quiz questions, flick to page 58 and tackle level three.

QUICK CROSSWORD

Our top puzzlers have concocted this crossword challenge especially for JB's most dedicated fans. Use the clues to help you work out the letters that fit in the blank grid below. If you get stuck, move on or flick through the annual pages to find the missing names, words or places.

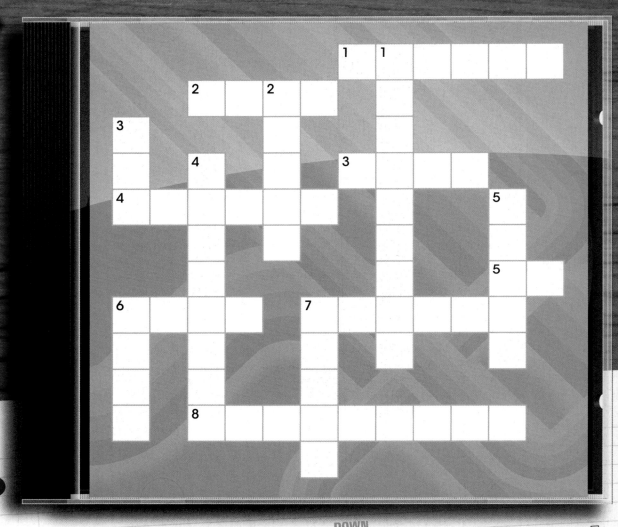

ACROSS

1. JB single about a happy facial expression.
2. A word to describe Justin now that he's made a lot of money.
3. Justin's biggest selling hit to date.
4. A dance move that Justin likes performing on stage.
5. Initials of the US city where Biebz played Madison Square Garden.
6. A loud type of music that Justin used to play when he was learning the guitar.
7. The first name of Mr Bieber Snr.
8. What fans at JB concerts can't help doing.

DOWN

1. The town where Justin grew up.
2. The first name of the artist who collaborated with Bieber on 'Up'.
3. As Christians, JB and his mum strongly believe in ___.
4. The name of the rapper featured alongside Justin on 'Baby'.
5. The first name of the artist who tweeted that Justin is his 'beat protégé'.
6. The name shared by one of Justin's best friends and his stylist.
7. The first name of JB's friend and star of *The Karate Kid*.

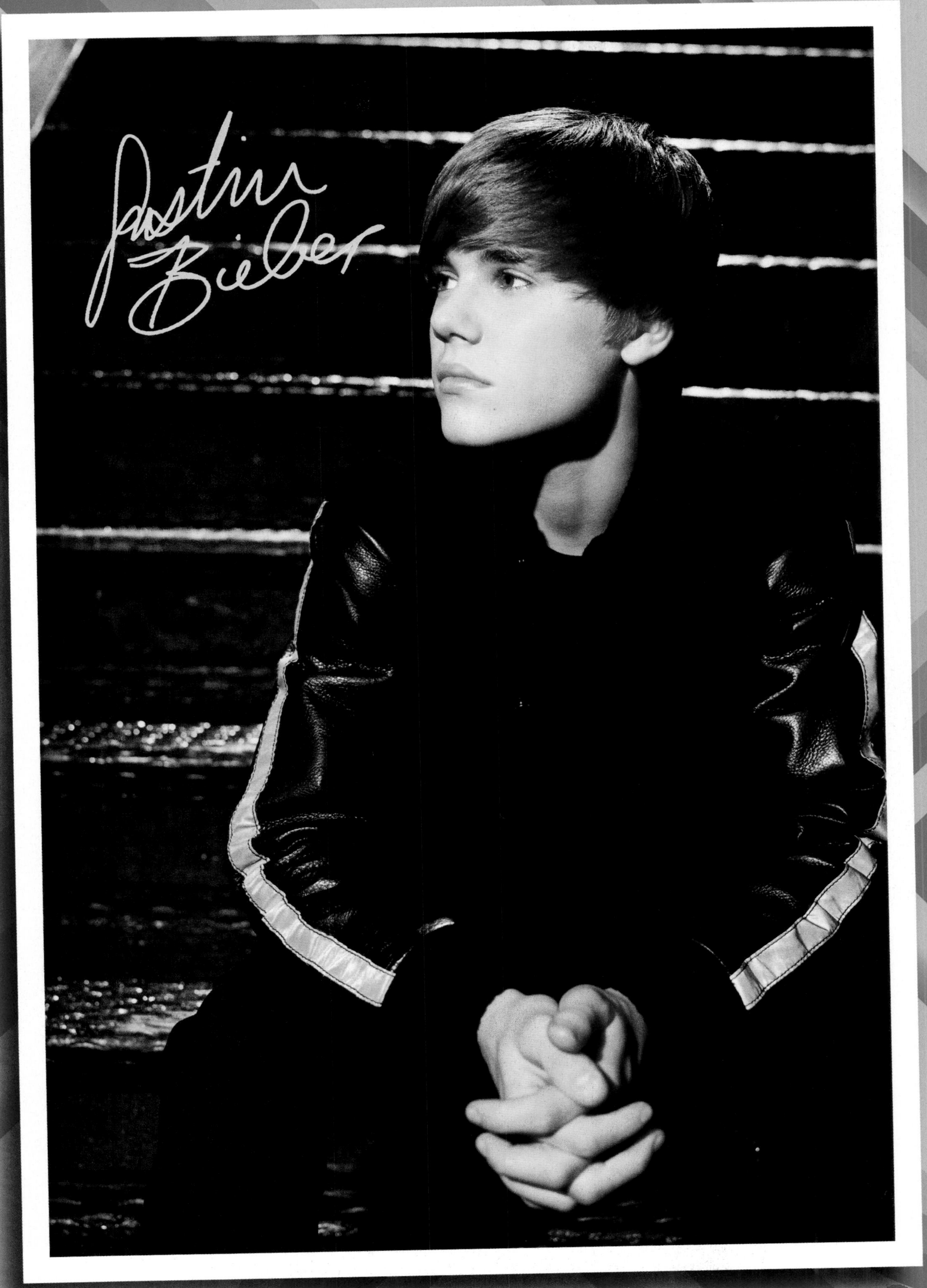
Justin Bieber

ALWAYS A WINNER

NEVER MIND THE COUNTLESS NOMINATIONS, WITH ALL THESE GONGS TO HIS NAME JUSTIN'S GOING TO NEED AN EXTRA HOME JUST TO DISPLAY HIS TROPHIES! HERE ARE SOME OF THE TOP MUSICAL PLAUDITS THAT THE IDOL HAS PICKED UP SO FAR...

2010

American Music Awards	Artist of the Year
	Favourite Pop/Rock Male Artist
	T-Mobile Breakthrough Artist
	Favourite Pop/Rock Album: 'My World 2.0'
Meus Premios Nick Awards	Favourite International Artist
MTV Brazil Music Awards	International Artist
MTV Europe Music Awards	Best Male
	Best Push Act
MTV Video Music Awards	Best New Artist
Much Music Awards	UR Fave: New Artist
	UR Fave: Canadian Video: 'Baby'
	International Video of the Year by a Canadian: 'Baby'
Myx Music Awards	Favourite International Video: 'One Time'
Teen Choice Awards	Male Artist
	Breakout Artist: Male
	Choice Summer Music Star: 'Male'
	Choice Music Pop Album: 'My World 2.0'
TRL Awards	Best International Act
Young Hollywood Awards	Newcomer of the Year

Brit Awards	International Breakthrough Artist	*2011*
Juno Awards	Fan Choice Award	
	Pop Album of the Year: 'My World 2.0'	
Nickelodeon Kid's Choice	Favourite Male Singer	
	Favourite Song: 'Baby'	
Billboard Music Awards	Top New Artist	
	Top Social Artist	
	Top Streaming Artist	
	Top Digital Media Artist	
	Top Pop Album: My World 2.0	
	Top Streaming Song (Video): 'Baby'	
CMT Music Awards	Collaborative Video of the Year:	
	'That Should Be Me' feat. Rascal Flatts	
MTV Movie Awards	Best Jaw-dropping Moment:	
	Justin Bieber: *Never Say Never*	

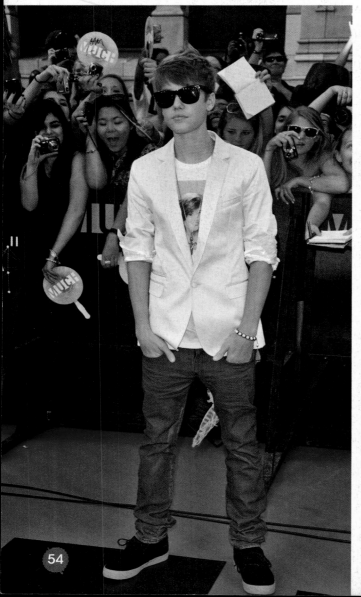

style it up

JB's laid-back look is all his own. Like all stylish teens, the star knows what works for him! Justin pairs simple staples such as checked lumberjack shirts, hoodies and cool tees with the latest baseball caps, dog tags and shades.

On tour, Justin keeps things interesting by making several costume changes during every show. Are you ready to channel your inner fashionista? Use this space to design an awesome outfit for the star that's head-to-toe hip!

THE BIG BIEBER QUIZ

LEVEL THREE

Hey! You've reached the final level of The Big Bieber Quiz. There's next to nothing you don't know about the man himself – or so you think. To achieve super-fan status you'll need to ace the questions below. Pick up a pen and get your head in the game. See you on the other side!

QUESTION 1

What went wrong on Justin's first date?

QUESTION 2

Which record label did Justin sign with?

QUESTION 3

What is the name of the venue where he did his first singing showcase?

QUESTION 4

Which city did Justin move to with his mum shortly after getting a record deal?

QUESTION 5

What is the name of the rapper who is also represented by Scooter Braun?

QUESTION 6

Where was Justin recently spotted holidaying with Selena Gomez?

JUSTIN BIEBER

QUESTION 7

Name two of the singing stars Justin admits to having a crush on.

QUESTION 8

Justin loves drawing. Can you name the job he has said he'd like to do if he wasn't performing or playing professional hockey?

QUESTION 9

Which Aretha Franklin track did Justin sing in the 'Stratford Star' competition?

QUESTION 10

Which animated star appeared on a poster in JB's room at his grandparents' house and featured behind him when he sang 'With You' on YouTube?

QUESTION 11

Which popular item of girls' clothing does Justin dislike?

QUESTION 12

The death of which music legend kept Justin's first single out of the Top Ten in the US?

QUESTION 13

What are Justin's backing dancers called?

QUESTION 14

How many cities did Justin's world tour hit?

QUESTION 15

What does Ryan Good help Justin with?

QUESTION 16

What does Justin most love doing to his tutor, Jenny?

QUESTION 17

Can you name Justin Bieber's maternal grandparents?

QUESTION 18

What is JB's favourite book?

QUESTION 19

Which famous US TV crime drama did Justin have an acting role in?

QUESTION 20

What is Justin's YouTube posting name?

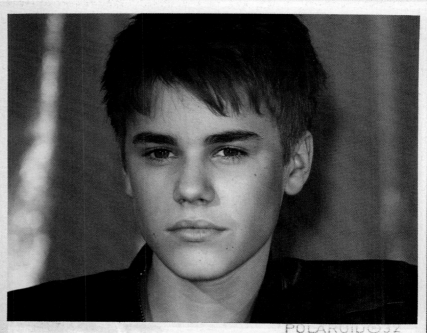

Wow! Your persistence has paid off. The fact you've finished every level shows that you're a true fan! Now check out your score. The answers are waiting on page 92.

YouTube
Yourself!

Want a piece of pop-star action? Justin's route to stardom shows it's possible to make success happen just by becoming a great self-publicist. If you've got a skill or talent, here's your 'how to' guide to sharing it with the world. Just remember to be web-savvy and ask a parent or guardian's permission before you post anything online.

YOU WILL NEED

- Yourself (and some friends)
- Your talent
- A willing friend or family member with a steady hand for filming
- A camcorder or phone with video function

WHAT TO DO

Star quality shines through even in the simplest clip – just look at the early ones of Justin singing his heart out in his bedroom. To let your talent do the talking, keep it simple. Find a quiet position in non-distracting surroundings where no one will walk past the camera, such as your bedroom or living room. Position yourself in front of the lens and get going. You may need to do several test runs before you get it right.

If you're really feeling über-creative, you could even film your own pop video. Take your fave Bieber track, listen to the lyrics and come up with a story to fit it, featuring your best mates in the starring roles. Or why not showcase your own dance moves to one of Justin's greatest hits?

GOING LIVE

When you're happy with what you've filmed, you'll need to log on to www.youtube.com. Instructions are all laid out on the site itself, but before you begin make sure your clip is smaller than 2GB in size, less than 15 minutes long and saved in an acceptable format. For a list visit YouTube – some of the most popular are WebM, .MPEG4, .AVI, 3GPP, .WMV and MOV.

Script it!

Use this space to plan out your clip, write down song lyrics or script the lines you'd like to say on screen.

COMING TO A CITY NEAR YOU!

BET YOU CAN'T WAIT FOR JUSTIN'S NEXT VISIT TO THE UK! IN THE MEANTIME, HAVE FUN IMAGINING WHERE THE GORGEOUS GUY MIGHT HOLD HIS NEXT GIG. FILL THE OPPOSITE PAGE WITH A KNOCK-OUT POSTER ADVERTISING THE BIEBZ' NEXT UNMISSABLE SET OF DATES.

STUCK FOR INSPIRATION?

- Think up a new name or tour theme – or put your own spin on the 'My World' Tour.

- Don't forget to list the dates and names of the places you'd like Justin to visit. He's playing your school hall? No way!

- Justin always has one or more supporting acts – the artist or band that takes the stage before him and warms up the crowd. The UK leg of Justin's tour featured special guest star Willow Smith. Who would you like to see open for JB next time around?

- Use your brightest colours and add bling with glitter pens to make sure that no-one will miss your poster creation when it's pinned on the wall.

BACKSTAGE PASS

TOURING SOUNDS GLAMOROUS AND IT'S CERTAINLY FUN, BUT THE EXPERIENCE FOR AN ARTIST IS ALSO GRUELLING. A GLOBETROTTING WORLD TOUR MEANS VERY LONG DAYS AND EVEN LONGER NIGHTS. HOURS AND HOURS ARE SPENT TRAVELLING BETWEEN VENUES ON BUSES AND PLANES AND OFTEN THERE'S NO TIME TO SEE ANY OF THE VENUE'S SIGHTS ONCE YOU GET THERE. DESPITE ALL THIS THERE'S ALWAYS A LIGHT AT THE END OF THE TUNNEL – THE AMAZING OPPORTUNITY TO PERFORM LIVE IN FRONT OF LEGIONS OF FANS!

JUSTIN'S TOUR JARGON

CATACOMBS
Dark corridors beneath the stage.

CATWALKS
Steel girders and beams that crisscross just beneath the roof.

FLY RIGGERS
Crew members who set up the harnesses and equipment so that Justin can fly above the audience.

GROUPIES
Die-hard fans who often follow Justin from country to country and would do anything to meet him.

EIGHTEEN-WHEELERS
Huge trucks that contain all the stage and set equipment.

PRE-PERFORMANCE RITUAL
The moment when JB huddles up with his crew before going on stage every night. This always includes a pre-performance prayer by Justin's youth pastor and a Jewish prayer introduced to him by manager Scooter.

RIDER
The list of things JB asks for in his dressing room.

ROADIES
The guys who set up the stage and equipment at each gig then pack it all up again afterwards ready for transportation to the next venue.

SET LIST
The numbered order of songs JB will perform on stage that evening.

TOUR BUS
The massive coach or coaches that carry Justin and his entourage from city to city, venue to venue.

JB loves touring, but just what does he get up to on the road? When he's not rehearsing or performing, the heartthrob can be found...

- Sleeping
- Chowing down on pizza
- Playing on his Xbox 360
- Pranking his crew
- Riding around the venue on a two-wheeled Segway
- Having water pistol battles
- Playing with his yo-yo
- Surprising die-hard fans who've camped out with tickets
- Studying with his tutor Jenny
- Tweeting his latest news, photos and antics
- Meowing like a cat and snorting like a horse – sounds he has to perform like musical scales, for his vocal warm-up.

BACKSTAGE DOWNTIME

THE VIDEOS

Ever wanted to know where JB's fab videos were shot, what the concepts were and which lucky girls got to cosy up to the Biebz? Read on for the inside scoop on some of Justin's most famous vids.

'BABY'

Filmed in a bowling alley, the boy-tries-to-impress-girl story was inspired by Michael Jackson's 'Way You Make Me Feel' video. The girl in 'Baby' was talented teen singer Jasmine Villegas. One of the shots involved Justin being spun round and round – he got so dizzy that he tripped over when filming finished! Canadian singer and rapper Drake turned up on the day to show his support for JB.

'NEVER LET YOU GO'

Shot on location in the stunning Atlantis Paradise Island Resort in the Bahamas, this video featured dolphins, crystal clear waters and Justin bouncing on an enormous bed. The girl he was courting here was actress Paige Hurd. Jealous, much?

'ONE LESS LONELY GIRL'

This hit was shot in a small, quaint outpost called Watertown. Justin was filmed sitting in the coffee shop, checking out the newsstand and playing with some pet-shop puppies. Unfortunately during the first take there was a slight mishap when one of the puppies had an accident on JB's foot. Awww!

'ONE TIME'

JB hit the jackpot with the video for this number, his very first track. The concept involved him hanging out with real-life best bud Ryan Butler and then throwing an enormous party in Usher's house. Cue lots of shots of the Biebz dancing and chatting up cute model and actress Kristen Rodeheaver.

'SOMEBODY TO LOVE'

Supremo Dave Meyers, the talent behind videos for Pink, Britney Spears and Shakira, directed this fantastic studio-based shoot. He chose to focus on JB and Usher's moves, bringing in backing dancers from top crew the Beat Freaks. Justin even got to show off his BMX skills, riding backwards while perching on the handlebars.

'EENIE MEENIE'

JB again got to hang out in the sunshine, this time in a Beverley Hills condo. The storyline featured JB and Sean Kingston being played by the same girl – the lucky model was chosen because she looked right for both Kingston – then aged twenty, and JB – then sixteen. Rapper Lil Romeo, singer Jasmine Villegas and Justin's friend Christian Beadles all made appearances, too.

FAMILY TREE

Family is everything to Justin. He credits his nearest and dearest with keeping him grounded when the world around him gets too crazy to handle. How familiar are you with JB's background? Grab a pen and fill in the Bieber family tree, using the names listed below.

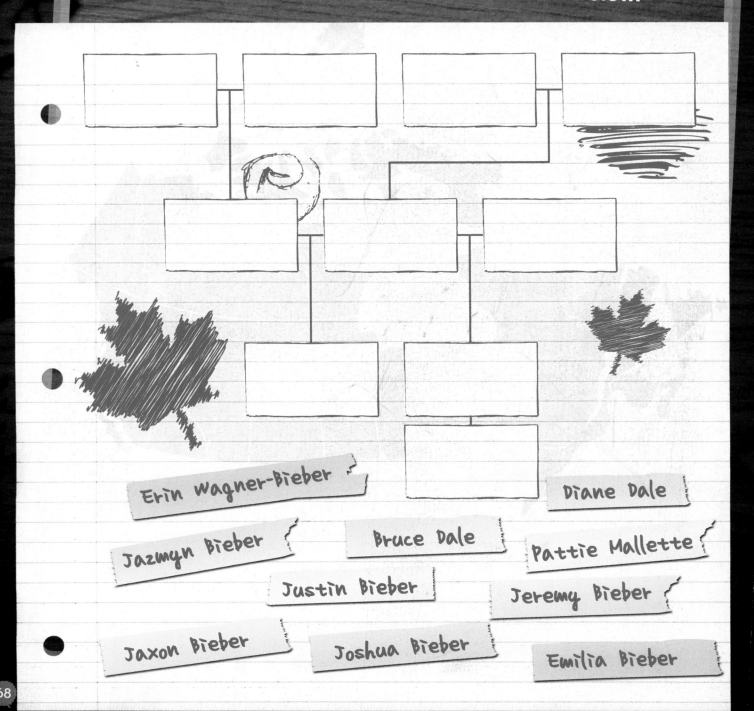

Erin Wagner-Bieber

Diane Dale

Jazmyn Bieber

Bruce Dale

Pattie Mallette

Justin Bieber

Jeremy Bieber

Jaxon Bieber

Joshua Bieber

Emilia Bieber

iPod, YouPod, WePod

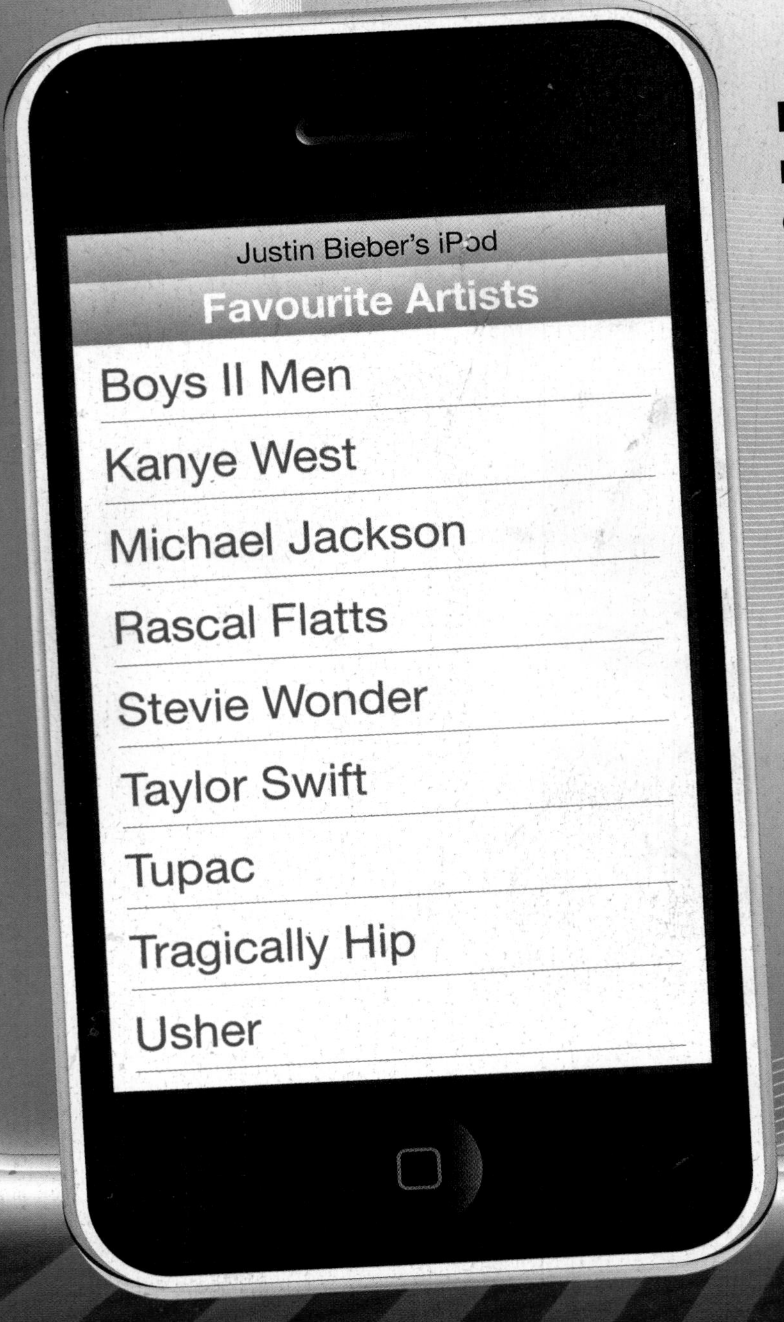

Justin Bieber's iPod

Favourite Artists

Boys II Men

Kanye West

Michael Jackson

Rascal Flatts

Stevie Wonder

Taylor Swift

Tupac

Tragically Hip

Usher

Biebz is a huge music fan and is constantly open to discovering new sounds, groups and artists. He just loves it when he gets asked what's on his iPod! Tune in to some of the great musicians who've inspired JB and then fill in the names of the artists who'd make it onto your MP3.

My iPod

Favourite Artists

WHAT MAKES A POP STAR?

S is for swagger and star quality, the unique assets that make an audience connect with you on stage.

P is for persistence. The music industry is a tough business – to succeed you need to focus, believe in yourself and never give up.

T is for talent. You're going nowhere fast without it, so zone in on what you're good at – singing, dancing or playing an instrument – and practise hard.

O is for opportunities. You'll need stacks of these in order to show the industry movers and shakers just what you can do. With hard work and determination you can create your own breaks, just like Justin did.

A is for adaptability. All the best and most enduring artists change their look and their sound to suit tastes and times. Think of Madonna or Gaga's chameleon-like qualities. Don't be scared to shake things up from time to time.

P is for personality. It's no good looking great if you've got nothing to say for yourself and no sense of humour. The most popular stars – including Biebz – have all these things in abundance.

R is for rhythm. You've got to have it, because these days pop stars need to be multi-taskers who can pull off killer dance moves as well as sing.

Bieber

BY NUMBERS

2

The number of episodes of the TV show *CSI: Crime Scene Investigation* that JB has appeared in.

4

The age at which JB got his first drum kit.

12

How old Justin was when he entered the 'Stratford Star' talent contest.

14

The number his first single 'One Time' peaked at on iTunes. It was kept from a higher position because Michael Jackson died the same week and his many hits flooded the chart.

86

The cities that Justin's 'My World' tour has visited.

2,000

The number of copies of his book that JB autographed for fans during a marathon signing session in New York City in 2010.

25,000

The amount of money (in pounds sterling) that a lock of Justin's hair fetched when auctioned on eBay! The cash went to an animal charity, but who paid that much for it?

31,000

The approximate population of Justin's hometown of Stratford, Ontario, Canada.

70,000

The people that JB actively follows on Twitter.

80,000

The outraged fans who stopped following JB on Twitter when he cut his hair.

900,000

The copies that 'My World' sold in the first five weeks after its release.

11,000,000 AND COUNTING...

The number of JB's Twitter followers.

61,000,000

The amount (in pounds sterling) that JB's movie *Never Say Never* has grossed worldwide.

PUT TOGETHER YOUR OWN

TOP POP ACT

IF YOU'VE ALWAYS DREAMED OF PERFORMING BUT DON'T WANT TO GO SOLO, THEN WHY NOT GRAB YOUR GIRLS AND PUT TOGETHER A GROUP? THE EXPERIENCE OF PERFORMING CAN BE EVEN MORE FUN WHEN IT'S SHARED WITH FRIENDS, PLUS YOU'LL HAVE THEIR SUPPORT IF THINGS GET TOUGH OR YOU LOSE YOUR VOICE. OVER THE NEXT FOUR PAGES WE'LL TALK YOU THROUGH EACH STAGE OF THE PROCESS, FROM SELECTING YOUR UNIQUE STYLE AND SOUND TO SETTING UP SCENE-STEALING PERFORMANCES.

CREATING A GROUP

PICK 'N' MIX
In a successful group it's important that you're all comfortable with each other, so you could choose your BFFs and get going straight away. But don't forget that music is a great way to meet new people, too. Maybe there are other people at school or in your local clubs who have talent. Get chatting to the girls in your dance class, swimming club or scout group and see if a collaboration comes together.

KEEP IT IN THE FAMILY
Perhaps you have an untapped source of talent even closer to home. Have you thought about your siblings or cousins? Many successful artists started out singing with a relative, growing their act from there. Think Jonas Brothers, NDubz, the White Stripes and Kings of Leon.

DUO OR SUPERGROUP?
How many people do you want in the group? The fewer of you there are, the fewer opinions you'll have to consider, but it might be easier to make decisions as a band. The more people, however, the bigger the talent pool and the richer the sound.

ROCK 'N' ROLE
Your personality types will play a big part in deciding which roles you'll take within the group. Extroverts may yearn to take centre stage whilst shy types will probably be happier doing backing vocals or playing an instrument.

HOLD AUDITIONS
This is a good way to see what you can all do. They don't need to be formal, you could just pick a song you love, arrange a get together and perform it individually and together. That way you can check you're in tune, see who plays which instruments and listen to the way your voices fit.

SETTING YOUR STYLE

Keep it real
Be led by your style – not the other way around. You need to feel comfortable when you're performing, so don't try fitting yourselves into slinky girl-band gear if at heart, you're all indie chicks or boho babes.

Get inspired
Think about the fashion that excites you and take inspiration from that. What floats your fashion boat? Do you love the military look or are you obsessed with vintage? If you're not sure, flick through magazines or watch your favourite bands on TV to get ideas.

Blend and separate
Bands often create a look or theme to the way they dress and then let each member give it their own twist. Maybe you could all go for a LBD in different styles or choose one denim piece each, such as a skirt, jeans or a jacket.

Name it!
The name of your group is crucial – it has to fit with your style and the kind of music you're going to be performing. Your name should be unique and meaningful to you, but it should also be something that trips off the tongue. Try holding a brainstorming session where you write down anything that comes into your head, then see which suggestions work best.

GET YOUR SOUND

Pick a genre

Is there a style of music you all particularly like? Are you pop stars, rock goddesses or country gals? If you're not sure, get together with your music collections and listen to as many different tunes as you can until you find a sound you all love.

Covers or original material

Although it may seem easier to sing existing songs, you'll need to put your own spin on them to make your performance work. If you are naturally musical you may prefer to have a go at writing your own songs. Pick the notes out on your instrument and keep a notebook around so you can write down lyrics as they pop into your head.

Mash it up

Why not take two or three songs you like, then weave them together in a brand new track, à la Glee? Mix things up by using the verses of one song and the chorus of another.

Can't hold a tune?

Give rapping a try – you can make great music with edgy lyrics and a brilliant beat. If you try dance or hip-hop, there are plenty of roles to go around, too. One of you can MC, one can beat box, one can lay down the tracks and another can sing the hook.

STEALING THE SCENE

Dress rehearsals

Before you launch yourselves onto the world, iron out any issues by performing some rehearsal gigs in front of your close family and friends. Ask them for some honest feedback and be prepared to listen to their views.

Playground power

This is a great way to get used to appearing in front of crowds. Why not start by giving impromptu performances during break time? It'll entertain everyone and allow you to gauge their reactions.

School productions

Don't pass on any opportunity to perform! Offer to sing at the school fête, in assembly or at the end-of-term show.

First gigs

It's best to start locally. Could you perform in your local park or shopping centre, or at the annual carnival or fair? You could offer to work with a local charity and raise money as you perform – that way you'll get an even bigger high!

PUT TOGETHER YOUR OWN

TOP POP ACT

BE STREET SMART!
Never busk outside without first gaining permission from your parent or guardian. You may also need a permit from the local council to busk in your area.

ONLINE APPEARANCE
For a guide to posting on YouTube turn back to page 60, although you'll need to get permission from everyone's parents before you do this. Remember that strangers online can be harsh with their criticism! If you're well-rehearsed and thick-skinned, however, this can be a great way to get yourselves seen.

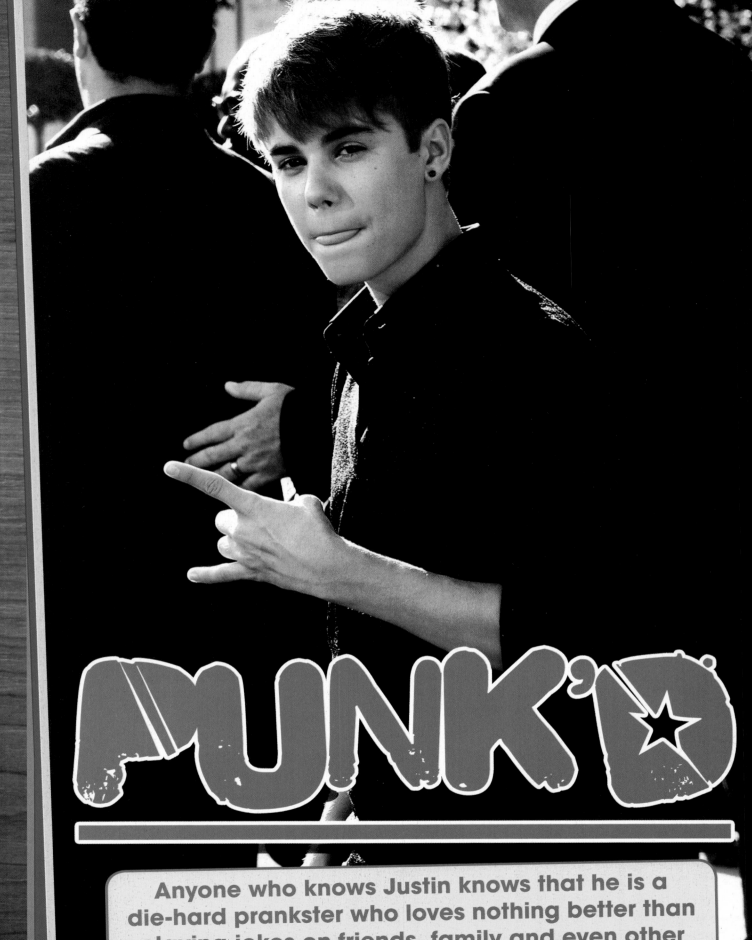

PUNK'D

Anyone who knows Justin knows that he is a die-hard prankster who loves nothing better than playing jokes on friends, family and even other fellow artists. Here are some of his greatest 'hits'.

While opening for Justin in Manchester last year, Willow Smith got a shock when Justin, Scooter and Ryan Good stormed the stage pretending to be backing dancers. Scooter and Ryan were even wearing lipstick and fake hair, which they began to whip back and forth to fit in with Willow's lyrics.

"JUST FOR FUTURE REFERENCE, IF YOU HAVE TO ASK ME IF I'M BEING SERIOUS, I'M NOT."

✪ **The star also pranked Canadian band Burnham, when they opened for him in Toronto. Justin pelted them with hundreds of coloured balls as they played, in retaliation for Burnham filling JB's tour bus bedroom with 4,000 balls earlier on the tour.**

Bieber celebrated pal Wilson Warren's birthday with a practical joke. He posted Wilson's mobile phone number on his Twitter page and pretended it was his own, urging his fans to call him. Wilson was inundated with calls from Beliebers but luckily saw the funny side, tweeting "Still friends. For now. Hahahaha."

Tutor Jenny is constantly on the receiving end of JB's jokes. Her star student once told her that he knew a cool science experiment which showed that if you put salt on top of butter it heats it up. In the name of education JB poured salt on a pat of butter and got Jenny to wait for sixty seconds for the chemical reaction to heat it up. As she hovered her palm over the butter trying to feel the non-existent warmth, tricky Biebz squished it down into the goo!

"PRANKS VS. SCHOOL: PRANKS WIN ALL DAY. CAN YOU BLAME ME? I'M JUST A KID."

Justin's guitarist Dan Kanter also fell foul of the Biebz when JB hacked his Twitter page and tweeted 'Hey guys just wanted to inform all of the fans first that I have resigned from working with Justin.' An hour later Bieber tweeted 'You will be missed @dankanter... but what you did was horrible. You will never be forgiven.' Naughty boy!

✪ **On April Fools' Day while on tour in Denmark, JB sent bodyguard Kenny Hamilton on stage to sing 'Baby'. He also pretended to buy comedy video website 'Funny or Die' which he renamed 'Bieber or Die'. He joked that he sometimes makes enormous people carry him around because he can't be bothered to walk, talks loudly in libraries and swims directly after eating because he doesn't care!**

Mum's the word

Sure he's a megastar, but as with any teenager Justin's mum Pattie has the final word. Here are just some of the tales that prove that Justin isn't above being put in his place if he steps out of line!

THE BOWLING INCIDENT

One night while they were in New York, Justin announced he was going bowling. His mum said that as it was already 10 p.m., it was too late, especially as he had to be in the hotel lobby by 6 a.m. The rest of the conversation went like this...

JMum: "Tonight's not a good night. You can go bowling any time."

JB: "Really? Any time?"

JMum: "All right. You name a time."

JB: "Ten o'clock?"

JMum: "That's too late, Justin. You're sixteen."

JB: "Exactly, I'm not two."

Justin didn't go bowling!

THE DRIVING INCIDENT

Justin and his mum had words over his sixteenth birthday present from Usher – a Range Rover. The problem was that Justin hadn't passed his driving test (you can drive at fifteen in the USA), but he was so keen to get behind the wheel he sneaked an illegal trip around the block. His mum went crazy, insisting that JB didn't drive until he'd got his licence. When he failed the test later that month he was so angry he refused to get in his mum's car. Instead he walked home in the rain with Pattie driving beside him.

"Mum travels with me. We argue, yes, I think every parent and son argue, but I love my mum. Sometimes I need a break because I'm with her 24/7, but I love her, I like being with her."

THE MIDNIGHT RUN INCIDENT

In an interview with the *Today* show, Pattie was asked about the worst thing Justin had ever done. She explained that before he was famous he sneaked out of the house at 2 a.m. to go bike riding with a friend. He was picked up by the police and brought home. His mum said, "I think it was good for him because it scared him and he never did it again."

THE MOBILE PHONE INCIDENT

Even JB's mum gets mad when her boy is constantly hooked up to his phone. Justin once said, "The other day she cancelled my phone plan. We got into an argument about something stupid, and she was like, 'Give me the phone' and I was like, 'No', so she just went and cancelled it."

THE LIPPY INCIDENT

When Biebz got lippy and disrespected his tutor Jenny during a car ride telling her to 'get back in her cage' while she was trying to talk to him about schoolwork, Mum stepped in. Pattie told Justin that his jibes weren't funny, saying that he should apologise even if he had been joking.

"Although I might not agree with her at the time, she's always right!"

TWEET MUCH?

WITH 11 MILLION FOLLOWERS, Justin is the second most popular Twitterholic in the Twitterverse! He ranks just behind Lady Gaga, but in front of Barack Obama and Britney Spears. Incredibly Justin also follows over 100,000 other Twitterers, keeping him connected with his fanbase. JB's tweets give amazing insight into his thoughts and feelings on life, love, friendship, fans, work and everything in between.

Tweets   Favourites   Lists ▾   Following ▾   **Followers**

Doctor came to see me this morning for my physical... took some blood. #notfun

Some days you are the bug: some days you are the windshield.

#ilovemyfans, my friends and my family. I give all my blessings to God and appreciate all that i have and will never forget to give back.

Met a great fan named amber who didn't have a camera so I took it for her. Here's ur pic amber. Nice meeting you.

@BieberWhisper always ignore rumours... don't think I'm changing. I'm growing up but my love and connection with you guys isn't ever changing.

Let's make a change and help build schools 4 those that never had an education. I will personally come to the school that raises the most.

No one is gonna be perfect all the time. But we grow and learn from our imperfection. Can't ever let them bring you down. I owe that to y'all.

It's funny when I read things about myself that r just not true. Why would certain people take time out of their day to hate on a 16 yr old?

If I could RT, follow and reply 2 all of u I would. I'm beyond grateful 2 u 4 ur never-ending support and sticking by me and my music. Thanks.

It's about that time... RANDOM CHUCK NORRIS MOMENT: Chuck Norris does not style his hair. It lays perfectly in places out of sheer terror.

Hello girls... i think we should all hang out very soon... all of us... together... often.

MANCHESTER was one of the best shows ever. It was just FUN!! CROWD WAS HYPED!! THANK YOU and LET'S Do It Again Tomorrow!! #myworldtour

PEN A HIT
FOR JB

In the past he's sung about love, friendship and loss, but whatever the track, his lyrics are always emotional and personal. Can you write a sure-fire hit for the man himself? The best writers draw on their own experiences for inspiration – what has happened in your life to make you feel sad, angry or full of joy? Use those feelings to make sweet music.

TITLE:

WRITTEN BY:

Don't
forget to
design a
cover for
Justin's
new single!

LOOK AGAIN!

Is there a more satisfying way to spend your time than staring at gorgeous pictures of JB? Here's the perfect excuse to have a good old-fashioned gawp. Check out these photos. The one on the right is not exactly the same as that the left. Can you circle six differences between the two? The answers are on page 93 if you get stuck, but you might just want to keep on staring into Justin's eyes until you get them all!

[SUPER-FAN YEARBOOK]

Justin Bieber inspires true devotion among his fans, but there is a line between 'loyal fan' and 'total loon'. We've compiled some of the most out-there antics for this, the 2012 Super-Fan Yearbook.

Most likely to...
GET INJURED

The girl who attempted to get JB's attention at a book signing in Hollywood. Justin said, 'I've had a lot of crazy fan encounters. Basically a girl decided she was just going to stand in front of a bus. Kenny got out there and yelled at her to get out of the way so she got scared and ran off.'

Most likely to...
END IN TEARS

The fans who surged forward causing a crush which injured several teens in Sydney, Australia. Police and paramedics cancelled the concert due to take place on the harbour because the crowd got out of control, leaving thousands disappointed.

Most likely to...
GO BROKE

The New Zealand fan who bought a discarded bottle of fizzy water for £423 after Justin took a sip out of it.

Most likely to...
GET THROWN OUT

The girl who, during Biebz's July 5th concert at the Verizon theatre in Texas, decided she had to get closer to her hero and stormed the stage. Her moment of glory was brief, as she was bundled off before she got a kiss and then escorted out by security.

Most likely to...
GAIN SYMPATHY

The New Jersey high-school pupils who waited for three days in Rockefeller Plaza to see JB perform on the *Today* show. They held up a sign saying 'we missed our prom to see JB'.

Most likely to...
GO BALD

A young boy in British Columbia, Canada, who paid £108 to have his wavy auburn hair chemically straightened to look like JB's. Now he's fed up with girls constantly touching it.

DON'T STOP BELIEBIN'

wassup!
This is just the beginning.
Thanks for making a small
town kid's dreams come true. I
love you all. we are a family.
Never say never... dream big.

Love
Justin XXX

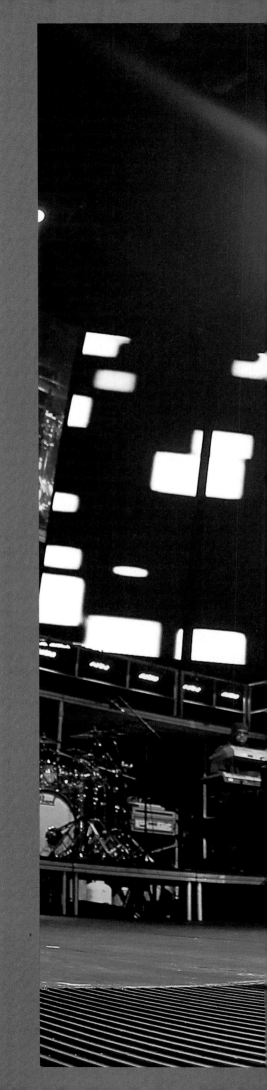

ANSWERS

PAGE 14: LEARN THE LYRICS

1. Are we an ITEM? Girl, quit playin',
'We're just friends', what are you sayin'?
C. BABY

2. I never thought I could feel this POWER,
I never thought that I could feel this free.
A. NEVER SAY NEVER

3. How many I told yous and start overs,
And SHOULDERS have you cried on before.
F. LONELY GIRL

4. When I met you girl, my
HEART went knock knock,
Now them butterflies in my
stomach won't stop stop.
E. ONE TIME

5. For you I'd write a symphony
I'd tell the violin,
It's time to sink or SWIM, watch
him play for ya.
B. SOMEBODY TO LOVE

6. There's a DREAM that I've been chasing,
Want so badly for it to be reality.
D. NEVER LET YOU GO

PAGE 16: WOLF PACK WORDSEARCH

U	G	F	E	A	B	C	R	Y	E
S	C	O	O	T	E	R	H	P	E
H	J	O	M	A	M	A	J	A	N
E	B	E	D	I	Q	U	K	T	X
R	Y	A	N	G	O	O	D	T	A
U	S	A	Y	N	A	W	P	I	R
S	D	W	V	X	Y	N	N	E	K
C	H	A	Z	S	O	M	E	R	S
R	E	L	T	U	B	N	A	Y	R
Y	J	A	M	A	I	C	A	N	K

PAGE 22: THE BIG BIEBER QUIZ – LEVEL ONE

1. False. He's Canadian.
2. False. He grew up in Stratford, Ontario, Canada.
3. True.
4. False. Her name is Pattie.
5. True.
6. False. His mentor is Usher.
7. False. It's ice hockey.
8. True.
9. False. It was called 'Stratford Star'.
10. False. It was 'One Time'.
11. True.
12. True.
13. False. It's spaghetti bolognese.
14. True.
15. False. It's Pisces.
16. True.
17. True.
18. True.
19. False. He broke his foot.
20. False. JB's eyes are brown.

PAGE 36:

In it or bin it?

Justin does not pet lion cubs, juggle melons, do the tango with Rhianna, swim naked in a lake, pilot his own private jet or shave Ryan's hair in the movie!

Who said it?

1. Chaz Somers / 2. Diane Dale / 3. Scooter
4. Mama Jan / 5. Justin Bieber
6. Chaz Somers / 7. Nathan McKay
8. Pattie Mallette / 9. Usher / 10. Scooter

PAGE 39: SAY WHAT?!

Justin has taken to Twitter to deny all these crazy rumours, apart from number 3. He is working on a film project with Will Smith's production company.

PAGE 44: THE BIG BIEBER QUIZ – LEVEL TWO

1. B / 2. A / 3. B / 4. B / 5. C
6. A / 7. C / 8. A / 9. B / 10. A

PAGE 46: QUICK CROSSWORD

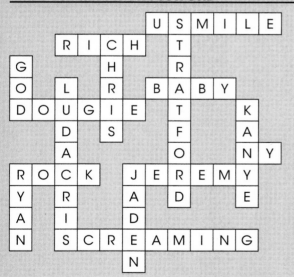

PAGE 58: THE BIG BIEBER QUIZ – LEVEL THREE

1. He spilled spaghetti down himself.
2. Island Def Jam (Music Group)
3. Eddie's Attic

4. Atlanta, Georgia
5. Asher Roth
6. Hawaii
7. Beyoncé, Rhianna
8. He has said he'd like to be an architect
9. Respect
10. Bart Simpson
11. Ugg Boots
12. Michael Jackson
13. Legaci
14. 85
15. He's a style and 'swagger' coach – he's also JB's road manager while on tour
16. Playing pranks on her
17. Bruce and Diane Dale
18. *Fledgling*, a Jason Steed adventure by Mark A. Cooper
19. *C.S.I.*
20. Kidrauhl

PAGE 68: JB'S FAMILY TREE

Emilia Bieber (paternal grandmother) and Joshua Bieber (paternal grandfather) had Jeremy Bieber (Justin's father). He and Pattie Mallette gave birth to Justin, but they are now divorced. Pattie's parents are Bruce and Diane Dale (Justin's maternal grandparents). Jeremy is now married to Erin Wagner-Bieber. The couple have Jazmyn and Jaxon (Justin's half brother and sister).

PAGE 86: LOOK AGAIN!

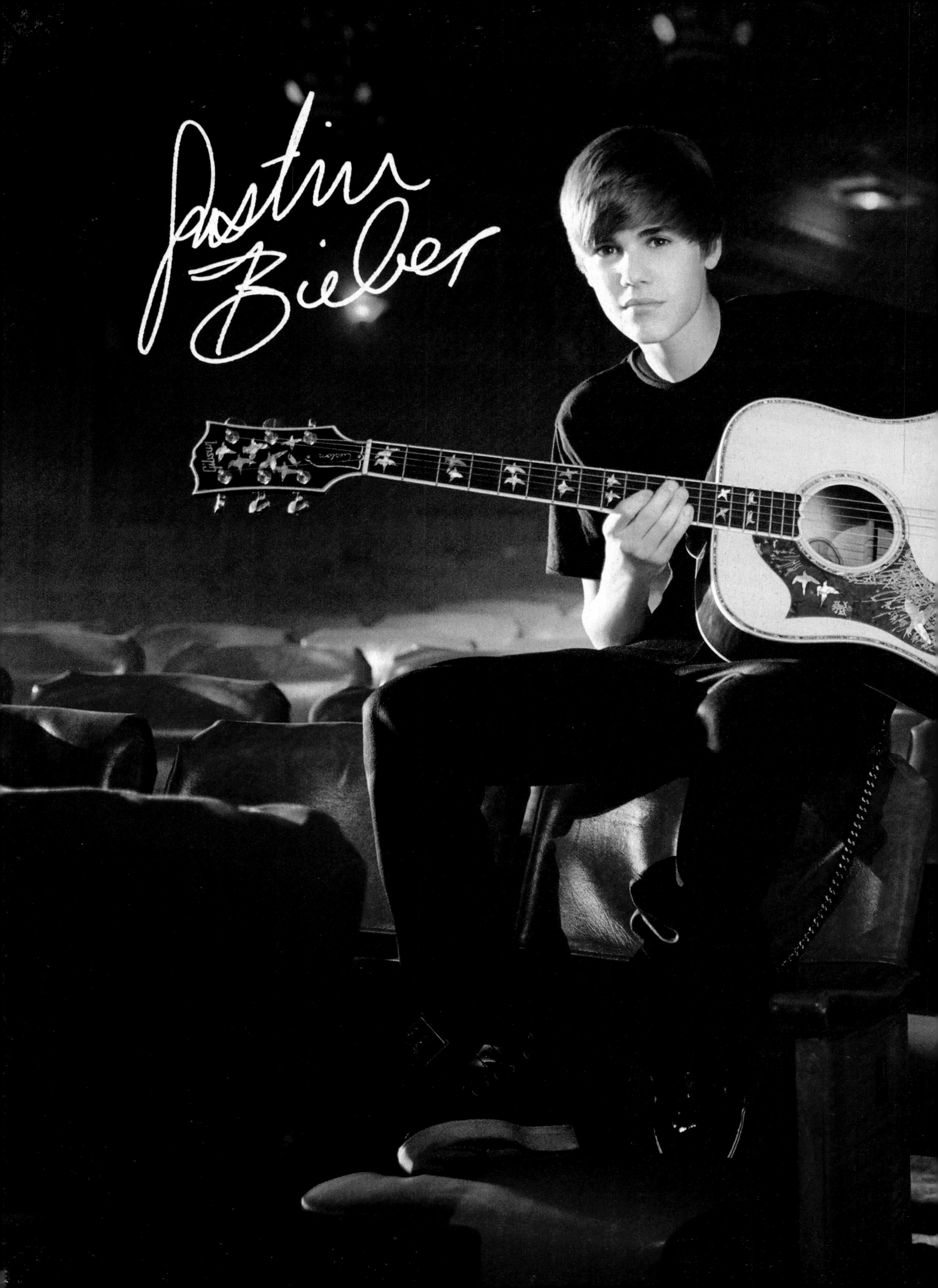
Justin Bieber